Famous Fake Photographs

Sally Odgers

Revised USA Edition © 2003 Published by Scholastic Inc.
By arrangement with Pearson Australia
(a division of Pearson Australia Group Pty Ltd).

Famous Fake Photographs
978-0-439-64881-3

Text copyright © Sally Odgers
Momentum Program Copyright © Pearson Australia 2010
(a division of Pearson Australia Group Pty Ltd)
First published 2003 by Reed International Books, Australia Pty Ltd

Fortean Picture Library/Cliff Crook: cover (top), p. 22; Rene Dahinden: pp. 23,
24, 25, 26, 27; Austin Hepburn: cover (middle), pp. 9, 10, 11, 12, 13, 14, 15, 16, 17,
18, 19; Marina Jackson: pp. 4, 6; Andy Radford: cover (bottom), pp. 28, 30; A.N.
Shiels: pp. 20, 21; Horizon Photo Library: p. 8; Bill Thomas: title page, pp. 5, 7, 29.

Printed in China (SWTC/04)

10 9 8 7 6 5 4   12 13 14 15

Contents

Introduction

A spirit photograph taken by Edouard Buguet.

Have you seen fairies in your backyard? Do you believe that the Loch Ness monster exists? Have you ever seen a ghost? Sometimes it is difficult to explain these events, but if you saw a photograph of a ghost on a staircase, you might be more likely to believe it.

We usually think of photographs as depicting the truth and how things really look. Yet, photographs can lie.

Fake Photographs

With the invention of the camera in the early nineteenth century, a whole new method of producing fakes was created. Art fakers had been painting false art works for a long time; many works of art had been copied and sold as masterpieces by art fakers. But no one suspected that fake photographs could be made.

When a person was photographed, it was assumed to be an exact record of how that person looked at the time the photograph was taken. But fakers were able to trick people by imposing other images on the photographs. They made the extra image look real, too. People believed that the camera did not lie, and fakers were able to use this belief to their advantage. Many fake photographs became part of a folktale or legend, like the Loch Ness monster, for example. People wanted to believe that it really did exist.

In 1991, two-year-old Greg Sheldon Maxwell began to say "Old Nana's here" and point up in the air. This photograph may show him looking at the ghost of his great-grandmother. Could it be real, or is it another fake photograph?

The First Faked Photographs

This photo is an example of a double exposure.

The first faked photographs almost certainly happened by mistake. Prepared glass or metal plates were used instead of film in the first cameras. If one of these plates was used twice, then two images would appear when the photograph was developed.

Later, when film was used in cameras, the photographer would take a picture, then wind the film on with a lever. This then brought a new piece of blank film into position. If the photographer forgot to wind the film on, or chose not to, then two photographs would be taken on the same section of the film.

This effect is called a double exposure because the same plate or piece of film has been exposed to the light on two different occasions. In a typical double exposure, a photograph of a house and a photograph of a person might share the same piece of film. The printed photograph might look as if a ghost were standing in front of the house.

Producing images side by side might make a slightly different kind of double exposure. In this way, a print could seem to show two people standing together, even if those two people had never met. A modern form of this photo magic was used in the film *Forrest Gump*, when actor Tom Hanks appeared to be shaking hands with President John F. Kennedy.

To the modern viewer, early double exposures are obviously either fakes or mistakes. To the people of the time, they were marvels.

Modern computer techniques are often used to produce photographs of things that look real, but which are actually impossible. This photo of a surfing polar bear is one example of these types of fake photographs.

Fake Ghost Photographs

This is the double-exposure photograph William Mumler accidentally took of himself. It shows the ghostly face of his cousin beside his own.

The first known ghost photographs were the first known fakes. William Mumler was an American engraver who was interested in the new invention of photography. In 1861, he discovered that the photograph that he had taken of himself was an accidental double exposure. Beside his self-portrait was a ghostly face. Mumler worked out the technique to duplicate this and developed a thriving business in spirit photography.

Another famous ghost photo is "The Brown Lady of Raynham Hall" in Norfolk, England. This ghost was first sighted in 1835 and is claimed to be the spirit of Dorothy Walpole, who once lived at Raynham Hall. Later, in 1936, a magazine photographer took this photograph. The fake has probably been created by a double exposure with the front image of the ghost out of focus.

The famous photo of "The Brown Lady of Raynham Hall," taken on September 19, 1936. The photographer was said to have seen an indistinct figure moving down the old staircase so immediately took the photograph.

Spirit Photography

During the late nineteenth century and early twentieth century, spiritualism was very popular. Spiritualists believed that the spirits of the dead could communicate with the living, especially through a person called a medium. Some mediums produced spirit photographs as proof of their ability to make contact with spirits.

This photo was taken by the medium Edward Wyllie in the late nineteenth century. It is supposed to depict some of the spirits he could contact. It is an example of the types of photos mediums took of themselves to prove their skills.

Many people were convinced that the ghostly image of a face in a photograph was that of a deceased relative or friend. Sometimes the spirit photographer would use old photographs of the deceased person to trick the customer. People were prepared to pay a lot of money for these photographs.

This is an example of a spirit photo taken around 1896. The woman whose ghostly image we see was probably supposed to be a relative of this man.

Spirit photography became very popular in America and England at this time. Reports of ghost sightings at that time were also common occurrences. The photographs were used as further evidence of the many reported sightings of ghosts and hauntings.

This photo of Estelle Stead, taken in October, 1915, by Mrs. Ada Deane, shows the image of Estelle's father, W.T. Stead, in the background. W.T. Stead died in the *Titanic* disaster in 1912. Estelle said she had never before seen a photograph of him like this one.

Exposing Fake Spirit Photographs

The spirit photo (left) taken around 1922 shows a Liverpool couple with their dead child. The photo to the right shows the child as he was around 1916.

At the beginning of the twentieth century, it was often easy to trace the original photograph that was used to create the spirit photograph. This was because photography was not as common as it is now. In the picture above, the spirit child photograph was proven to be taken from a painting that had been used as an advertisement many years earlier.

Many spirit photographers were shown to be frauds. William Mumler had become a famous spirit photographer, but in 1869 he was charged with fraud. Mumler was acquitted, but it is said that this was helped by the supporting testimony of a judge who believed in spiritualism. Mumler's famous "Ghost of Lincoln" photograph shows the image of the recently assassinated President Lincoln behind the portrait of a woman.

Fake Fairy Photographs

Two young cousins, Elsie Wright (sixteen years old) and Frances Griffiths (ten years old) took the famous fake fairy photographs. In 1917, the girls were playing in the woods near Elsie's home at Cottingley Glen, West Yorkshire, England. They took the photographs to convince their parents that fairies did exist. Later, in 1920, Sir Arthur Conan Doyle (the creator of Sherlock Holmes) showed great interest in them. The girls took three more photos for Sir Arthur, who was convinced that they were authentic.

Elsie Wright with a "fairy," photographed by Frances Griffiths at Cottingley Glen, West Yorkshire, August, 1920.

Because of their young age, no one believed that the girls could produce fakes. The cousins also claimed that they must be left alone to photograph the fairies, who of course only trusted them.

In fact, the girls photographed paper cutouts from a popular children's book of the time, *Princess Mary's Gift Book*. They stood up the cutouts with hatpins.

Frances Griffiths at Cottingley Glen, West Yorkshire, July, 1917, with the Cottingley fairies. The photograph was taken by Elsie Wright.

Exposing the Fake Fairy Photographs

Many people wanted to believe in the fairy photographs. Finally in 1983, Elsie, now eighty-two years old, and Frances, now seventy-six years old, admitted the hoax. If you study the photos closely, you can see that there is no fuzziness and the fairies are easy to see. In "Frances and the Dancing Fairies," the girl is looking straight at the camera, ignoring the cutout figures in front of her. In "Elsie and the Gnome," the girl's hand seems a very odd shape. It is actually a false one used as a stand to support the cutout gnome.

A "gnome" with Elsie Wright, photographed by Frances Griffiths, September, 1917. Notice the odd shape of Elsie's hand in this photo.

The fairy pictures were also probably retouched and improved by other photographers who made and sold prints of the photos.

These fakes show the powerful effect of photography that confirms what people want to believe.

A "fairy" with Frances Griffiths, photographed by Elsie Wright, August, 1920.

Fake Monster Photographs

Is this the Loch Ness monster? This photo, taken on August 11, 1996, by Austin Hepburn, shows an unusual wake on Loch Ness. It was a clear day with no wind and no boats were moving on the Loch.

The Loch Ness monster has intrigued people for centuries. The earliest reported sighting was by St. Columba around 565. Many people have visited Loch Ness in the search for the famous monster. There have been thousands of reported sightings of the Loch Ness monster and many photographs have been taken. This has increased in number since a road was built around the lake in 1933. However, there is still no convincing proof that the monster exists. It is easy to be tricked by other swimming animals, such as otters, or moving waterweed or driftwood. The water in the lake is very deep and dark, which makes visibility difficult.

Many photographers believe that the photographs that they have taken prove the existence of the monster. One famous photo known as the "Surgeon's Photograph" is well known because it was finally acknowledged to be a fake.

In 1934, Colonel Robert Wilson, a doctor, claimed to have taken a photo of the long head and neck of the monster rising out of the lake. In actual fact, the monster was made from plastic wood built up over the conning tower of a toy submarine. Many years later, in 1993, Christian Spurling explained how he and his stepfather, Duke Wetherall, faked the monster. Duke Wetherall was famous for his monster hunting and had been hired by a newspaper to investigate Loch Ness. He had been tricked by some fake footprints near the lake and decided to plan his own hoax in revenge. The fake monster was photographed and the pictures given to Wilson, who sold them to the very newspaper that had hired Wetherall for the initial investigation.

The famous "Surgeon's Photograph" of the Loch Ness monster, taken in April, 1934 by a London surgeon, R.K. Wilson.

Exposing the Fake Monster Photographs

The success of the hoax was quite overwhelming, and it was not until about sixty years later that Spurling disclosed the truth about the fake photograph.

Many people had suspected that the "Surgeon's Photograph" was a hoax, but others were convinced that scientific examination showed that the photograph of the Loch Ness monster was genuine.

Another photo of the Loch Ness monster. This one was taken by Anthony Shiels from Urquhart Castle, May 21, 1977.

Other Fake Creature Photographs

Monsters such as the Yeti or Abominable Snowman have also been photographed. It is possible to fake these pictures by taking photos of apes or bears or of people dressed up in monster suits. If the photo is blurred, then it is difficult to identify the subject.

This is supposedly a photo of Bigfoot. It was said to have been taken on July 11, 1995, by a forest ranger at Wild Creek in the Mount Rainier foothills in Washington State. Many Bigfoot researchers believe the photo is a hoax.

Fake UFO Photographs

There have been many reported sightings of UFOs, or unidentified flying objects. It is possible to explain some as photos of weather balloons, unusual light conditions, or odd-shaped clouds. However, other UFO photos are deliberate hoaxes. Objects such as flying Frisbees, plastic models, buttons, or plates have been photographed and recorded as UFOs.

A UFO over Venezuela. This photo was taken in 1963 by an Avensa Airlines pilot flying between Barcelona and Caracas. The pilot later admitted to a hoax; the UFO is actually a button.

In 1967, two American boys, Dan and Grant Jaroslaw, aged fifteen and seventeen, made a model of a UFO and photographed it. When their mother contacted the newspapers after seeing the photos, the fake was accepted as fact. Later in 1967, the boys explained that the hoax had gotten out of control.

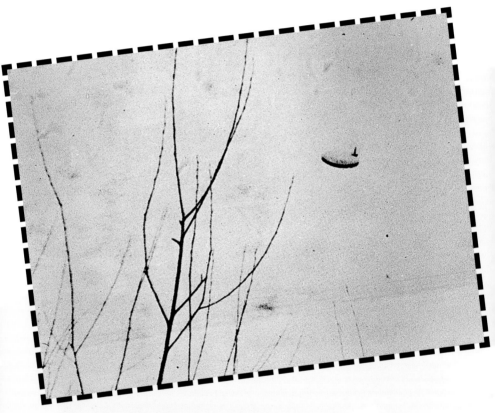

One of four fake UFO photos taken by the Jaroslaw brothers of Lake St. Clair, Michigan. The photos were taken on January 9, 1967. The brothers later confessed to a hoax.

The Roswell UFO crash in New Mexico, in 1947, is another famous UFO incident. There is a film of an autopsy performed on an alien figure that was claimed to have been rescued from the crashed spaceship. The wreckage of the "spaceship" was later explained to be that of a weather balloon.

In the photo below, Major Jesse Marcel, Intelligence Officer at Roswell Army Air Field, holds the remains of a "flying disk" in July, 1947. The remains were found that year on a sheep ranch in New Mexico. Marcel maintained that the material seemed "not of this Earth," but in fact it was probably the remains of a weather balloon.

Critics of the autopsy film claim that the corpse is the cast of a human being made when the person was standing up. Questions have also been asked about some of the objects in the background of the film.

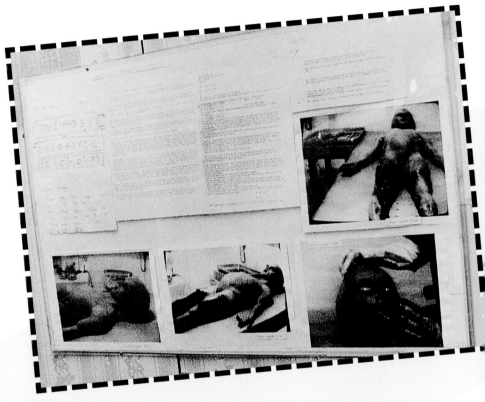

This display in a UFO museum at Roswell, New Mexico, shows photos that were taken at the supposed alien autopsy.

How Can You Tell a Fake Photograph?

Photo Patterson/Gimlin. © 1968 Dahinden

Fake photographs are often not very good quality photos. The gray and grainy pictures blur the outlines of the subject. For example, the running figure of Bigfoot or Sasquatch is not very clear. It is hard to verify that the figure is a female Sasquatch and not someone dressed up in an ape suit.

This is a frame from a movie of Bigfoot taken by Roger Patterson on October 20, 1967, at Bluff Creek in northern California. The film captured what the photographer claimed was Bigfoot running through the forest.

Spirit and ghost photos appear very fuzzy and faint. These photos are often taken at night or where there is poor lighting, which confuses the image.

Photographers who take fake photos often claim that they have to take the picture quickly. They have no time to adjust the lens or film speed. If, for example, the Loch Ness monster suddenly appeared, you would not expect the photo necessarily to be a clear, sharp image. The photographer would be excited and would take the photos in a hurry.

A photo of the Loch Ness monster, taken in November, 1933, by Hugh Gray. The photo is very blurry, as if taken in a hurry.

Artistic Photographic Fakes

There are also legitimate fake photographs. Artists combine different pictures photographically as works of art. Photographers can also retouch portraits, for example, by painting out shadows and tiny scars on the photos. Photographs we see on television or in magazines have often been retouched in this way.

This artist is touching up and adding color to these photos. This sort of legitimate fake photo is often used for special purposes, such as advertising or for decoration.

The Future of Fake Photographs

A UFO depicted by a model and trick photography.

As technology becomes more sophisticated, it is easier to produce fake photos. Modern digital cameras can produce realistic pictures of almost anything. People are used to and enjoy the special effects of films and trick photography.

Fake photographs can be fun. The hoaxes that have succeeded in the past were often done as jokes or experiments. Many people would like to believe in UFOs and ghosts. Photographs can confirm that belief and stir the imagination.

Glossary

authentic	genuine, true
autopsy	a medical examination of a dead body
conning tower	the tower built on top of a submarine that contains the periscope
depict	represent or describe
digital camera	a filmless camera that captures an image so it can be converted, downloaded, and manipulated by a computer
duplicate	copy
engraver	a person who cuts a design or lines on metal or wood from which to take prints
impose	lay or place
legitimate	lawful, proper, or regular
masterpiece	a person's best work
medium	a person who claims to be in contact with the spirits of the dead and to be able to communicate between the dead and the living
spirit photography	photographs of ghosts or fairies
spiritualism	a belief that the spirits of the dead can communicate with the living, especially through a person who is a medium

Index